Poetic Potions

Whispers Of The Soul

Merlyn Reena

/ BookLeaf
Publishing
India | USA | UK

Made with ❤ on the BookLeaf Publishing Platform
www.bookleafpub.in
www.bookleafpub.com

Dedication

To my beloved parents who always supported me, and to all my readers who seek solace, comfort, and wisdom in a book.

To my dad, who's always been loving and patient.

To my mom, my soulmate and working partner, and to my nephew, who's been a spark of light and a bundle of joy in my life.

Preface

This book was born out of my love for poetry and writing. It's all the whispers of my soul caught on paper.

When inspiration strikes me, I grab a pen and paper and jot down all that needs to be said, and that's how this book was formed.

This collection of poems is themed around life, love, and wishes fulfilled.

I hope you find what you're looking for.

Acknowledgements

I would like to acknowledge Book Leaf Publishing for helping me take the next step in my writing career, and my sincere thanks to the team for sending this out into the world.

1. When You Wish Upon A Star

Dreams do come true
When you wish upon a star.

Your soul's yearnings
Echo through the Universe.

Like a song travelling
Through space and time.

Your heart's wishes thunder
Through the fabric of reality.

Every wish carries a musical note
In the symphony of life's music.

And when you make a wish
Through silent whispers or open confessions.

The Universe listens

And answers your prayers.

For every earnest desire
Never goes unheard.

Dreams do come true
When you wish upon a star.

2. Ask The Soul

The soul knows best
Where to go, what to do.

It stirs up your heart
And pulls on your heartstrings.

For every soul has its purpose
And came here for a reason.

To live a life
As planned before lifetime.

The soul knows best
Where to go, what to do.

Simply follow its nudges
And you'll do just fine.

For the soul is never wrong
And knows the highest good.

When you're lost
And it's hard to see.

The soul knows best
Where to go, what to do.

3. The Prophecy

Who am I to change the prophecy?
To rewrite what's written in the stars?
Death and rebirth themes scream my name,
Like a Phoenix rising out of the ashes,
I have more than nine lives.

A watch ticking in my pocket,
Telling me, "It's time,"
To close the gate behind me,
And step into the daylight.
There once was a storm, but now clear skies.

I died more than once,
In my grave I lie.
Covered with ivy,
Waiting for my time.

Till the stone is moved,
And my lifeless body risen,
I lay in my sleep,

Patiently waiting.

I hear my guides whispering,
"Just one more time."
"She'll make the world a better place,"
"A better forever."

The evil witch cursed me with death,
But the good one blessed me with life.
When I die, I go to sleep,
Only to be raised by life's kiss.

An endless theme in my life chart,
To be blessed with endless luck.
Though darkness covers,
There'll always be light.

Here I am one more time,
To taste life's kiss,
And unravel the mysteries,
That runs the world from behind.

The heavens decide my fate,
Who I meet,
When I meet;
All my fated encounters.

It's mapped out in the skies,
What I'll do,
And where I'll be;
All the chapters of my life.

For the stars have the final say,
Not me and you;
On what happens,
And what happens not.

The constellations have stamped the contracts,
And have said their final words.
It's all recorded up there.
May you hold your peace.

A pattern imprinted for a life lived well.
At night, when you dream,
It's the heavens that communicate;
Whispering their secrets,
That you seldom know of.

They say,
"Know this, my little child,
That you'll always be heaven's first love,
We'll guide you and mentor you,
You'll forever be safe in our hands."

4. Blame Cupid

These tiny little cherubs are to be blamed!
Did Cupid unleash his magical golden arrow on me?
To melt my heart into a puddle?
To show me what love is,
To enjoy the pleasure of the haze.

The constellations devised their brilliant scheme.
Did the celestial bodies position themselves?
To align destinies?
To intertwine us?

Like a lovesick Cupid and curious Psyche,
This love made something magical,
From something mundane;
Something immortal from something mortal.

Does the everyday man even comprehend love?
Its depths?
Its volatile emotions?
The magic coursing through my veins?

Love is enough!
Love transcends the ordinary,
The entire Universe aids you,
With everything you need.

The winds blow in your favour,
The birds lead the way for you,
The flowers light the path for you,
The rabbits guide you as you go.

Love perseveres.
It helps you transcend all trials,
The impossible becomes possible,
For the gods helped her out.

True love transcends.
It never ends,
It only keeps flowing,
Like a never-ending river.

And when they see you,
Surpassing every obstacle on your way,
The gods intervene,
To unite you and pledge you to immortality.

Did she just alchemise?

A mortal princess of extraordinary beauty,
Into a powerful, immortal divinity?
The transformative power of a love potion!

And so it goes,
That the union of two souls of love,
Changed the mundane into magic.
A fairytale out of tragedy.

5. The Final Straw

Was I too patient?
The goddess protecting you,
During your lowest.
Did you bite the hand that fed you?
Did you take for granted,
My grace and power?

Did I do what you did to me?
Did it hurt because,
Now it was your turn?
Did I unleash my wrath on you?
The final straw.

Did I destroy us forever?
The ties - going up in flames.
And did I walk away,
Without a second thought?
Without any remorse?

I was your angel,

But now I can be the devil,
Did I let loose my female rage?
Walk away like it was nothing?
I was your guardian angel,
But now your very nightmare.

You'll find someone,
But it won't be me.
They'll love you for sure,
Skin-deep for sure.
Your clowns will approve of her,
But never really adore her.

You'll feel great,
A new chapter,
A new phase.
It will glitter till it stops,
It will be fun till it fades.

Then you'll know,
That you had the golden goose,
Right in your yard,
But killed it for greed's sake.

I was your answer,
I was your saving grace.
Now, you'll see,

How life will be,
Without me in it.

You prayed about this,
Midnights without sleep,
I was your candlelight,
But you let your smaller self slip.

I beared your tantrums,
Your pain; your hurt.
I was your very healing,
But you projected your hurt on me.

Did envy blind your eyes?
Did hatred engulf you?
Till you weren't thinking straight,
And destroyed the very thing,
That was supposed to be your medicine.

You poisoned the cup,
With envy and hatred,
When all I brought you,
Was my love potion.

Did you feel big?
After winning a match,
With someone not your size?

Now, I'll show you my divinity.
You'll see my power,
You'll beat your head in insanity,
Wondering why you did,
What you did to me.

I hope you find yourself,
And not lose yourself in this game.
Because I brought you love,
But you brought pain,
Because someone broke you.

Did your clowns clown you?
You thought they had your back.
But no, they were just after your stash.
Soon, you'll see,
That beneath their admiration,
Was an ultimatum.

You'll search the room,
For someone loyal and kind.
For someone who'll hold you,
Through thick and thin.
But you won't find them.

Because your lovers,
Had an ultimatum.

They'll love you till,
You dance to their tune.
They saw nothing in you,
When I saw the world in you.

They trashed pearls,
The typical way.
But funny, how you did the same.
Did what go around,
Come around?

Did you become the very person,
That caused you pain?
You let your bitterness,
Turn you into poison,
Instead of magic.

6. The Grand Play And Behind The Scenes

The world - the stage,
And the people you meet - actors.
How do you play the game?

The facade is grand,
And poetically brilliant.
The actors play their parts.

But when the lights fade,
And the show's over,
How do you feel?
In the pit of your belly?

He puts on a show,
Full of dazzling lights and wonder;
All smiles and merry.
He's on a winning streak.

But when the lights turn down,

And he's leaving home,
On his way, his sorrow creeps in,
Slowly and uninvited.

He can't shake off the void in his soul,
And the ache in his heart.
He did what the world asked of him,
But rarely what his soul wanted.

He's in the midst of a circus,
Surrounded by clowns,
Dancing and joking,
And smiling around.

But when he turns his back,
He knows he's failed his own soul.
The crowd's happy, but he's not.

He loves me,
And cannot shake off the feeling.
I've crept on him like an Ivy,
Onto a stone home.

The pull, stronger than ever;
The ache, palpable.
At night, when he sleeps,
All he feels is this void,

That keeps sinking in his chest.

It's meant to be, but maybe not.
Maybe I'll stay with him as a phantom,
Haunting his thoughts and dreams.

Maybe I'll be his muse,
That got away, never to come back.
The mother of his creations,
In his head, but absent,
When he looks around.

Who are you living for?
At night, he rests,
Knowing at least someone's happy -
His mother, father, and his circus clowns.

Maybe one day, it will be his turn.
He can live life for himself,
And not for others.

Maybe he can make himself,
And others, happy,
If he keeps walking down,
His soul's path.

7. Dear Nephew

Dear Nephew,
You've been my love and light,
Since the day you took,
Your very first breath.

Your laughter and cries,
Fill this room with memories,
Of you being completely yourself.

You're the cutest thing,
I've ever seen.
You're one of a kind;
A joy in my life.

I feel complete with you,
By my side.
You fill every void,
I've ever had.

You're God's boon,

To me and the family.
Your smile lights up the room.
Your animated giggles,
Brightens up my day.

You and me,
We share the same bond.
Like we've known each other,
For lifetimes.

I'll always be your cornerstone,
A hand to hold, no matter what.
You'll always be my special love.

Love,

Your Godmother.

8. Shades Of Blue

When I met you,
I was all shades of blue.
My skies were grey-blue,
And my soul, cold as ice.

I was frozen -
Frozen in time.
Lips, blue from the frost,
Face, pale from the cold.

My heart, cold as ice,
Thumping blood,
To keep my ice-cold body,
A warm-blooded human.

Hopes forever gone,
I knew it was over.
Then, I saw you for the first time,
Wearing a warm smile,
And an ice blue shirt.

At that moment, I knew
That this was just the beginning.
I met you at the ripe time,
But in the wrong weather.

It's a winter storm,
And everywhere I look,
Something's dying.

My face hasn't seen colour,
In a long time.
My rose poudre blush,
Slowly fading.

I look around and I see,
The cold scene.
But then, I see you,
And I know, I'll be just fine.

I'm embracing this blizzard,
These icy winds,
And the winter storm.
I'm embracing the weather;
I'm welcoming the hailstorm.

Because I know I'll be standing tall,

And do more than just fine,
Because I just found,
My soul lover.

So, I'll be dancing
Through the hailstorm,
And singing
Through the squall.

And I won't wait
For the weather
To pass by.

Because it's you and me,
Through thick and thin.
Stuck together,
Through it all.

9. To My Grandpa

To my Grandpa on the Other Side,
Your love is like a light shining
In the darkness.

You've shown me the way
With your compassion.
Your warmth fills my heart.

Your stories of how you grew up;
Your teachings on life,
Paved the way for me.

Your kindness and compassion
Showed me that strength
Does not have to be brutal -
It can be subtle and gentle.

You lead the way with your conduct.
Your moral compass
Always guides me.

I'll make your heart swell with pride,
I'll live the dreams
Of every ancestor before me.
I vow to make it all count.

I know you'll always be guiding me
Through the day and the night,
With signs and dreams and angel numbers.

Your prayers for me
Has made me into who I am today.
Your blessings will carry me
Through this life path.

Love,

Your Granddaughter

10. A Wedding In The Cosmos

So I said,
"Take me away to a distant planet.'
"Let's go stargazing into outer spaces."

I'll love you to the moon and to Mercury.
Let's make our home between celestial bodies.

Let's have our wedding in the Cosmos,
Where all the planets,
And the dieties can join in.

It'll be a day to remember.
A story marked in the skies.

Where fates are merged
With lifetimes spent together.

And we'll bear children
Who'll freely saunter the Elysian Fields.

A life imbued with love and stars
And cosmic dust.
Forever into eternity.

11. Magic

Crystal balls, tarots, and magic potions
Couldn't do what you did.

Your love brought me to life -
The perfect alchemy.

Like the asleep rising from life's kiss.
Your heart awakened mine.

And I don't need a sorcerer
When you perform the perfect wizardry.

I don't need an occultist
You're all the magic I could ever need.

And I don't need incantations
Your spell works just fine with me.

Your enchantments are all the charms
That I'll ever need.

Your trinkets protect me from all harm.
Your amulet ring protects me from all devilry.

Your talisman chain brings me good fortune.
Your necromancy brought me to life.

Your occultism and esoteric mysticism
Is my gnosticism.

You illuminate me with your mentalism
And enlighten me with your sleight of hand.

Your love is the only magic potion
I'll need to partake of.

12. This Love

This love is like the vast ocean
Meeting the skyline.

Widespread, tame,
With a chaotic undercurrent.

We love with a passion,
And hate with an even more fixation.

Just like the ocean
That can be calm and tame.

But also, perturbed and flustered
At the same time.

Our love is as deep
As the ocean depths.

The deep sea we dive,
The more our world opens up.

Kingdoms unknown, unseen,
And unheard of;

Lifeforms of all kinds;
Habitats and ecosystems.

The more time flows,
The more we love each other.

Chaos settling into calm,
Serene and tranquil waves.

We get each other now.
We understand each other.

Our bond goes way deeper
Than skin-deep.
More like soul-deep.

I know now that this love -
It will never end.

It's as vast
As the ocean spans.

Our devotion to one another

Will take us deeper
And make us stronger.

This lifetime,
And lifetimes to come.

13. House Of Cards

His life was like a house of cards.
He had the perfect deck,
But he squandered it.

He's built a life on lies,
And that's why it crashes,
Every single time.

Just give it time.
When the ship rocks,
It's all gonna collapse.

The hand he was dealt
Was lucky.
He hit the jackpot.

But how he played his cards
Was misery.
He played it poorly.

And soon the storm hit,
As it always does,
To test the foundations
And reward the players.

His house of cards
Lay flat, from the wind.
He got it all wrong.

Life is how you play
With the cards you're given.
You can make good from bad
And bad from good.

So he puts his hands
In his head.
Cries in sorrow.

But he does not get why
It never worked out.
He was dealt a good hand
But he played it abysmally.

And he got what he earned,
Just and fair.
Because that's how he
Chose to play it.

14. Lunar Magic

I keep my eyes on you.
Your waxing and waning.

Do your lunar magic!

I write my spells
And say my prayers
On a new moon.

As you grow,
The tides get stronger
And my will gets fierce.

I release my powers
And work on my potions.

Do your lunar magic!

Your lunar cycles
Are my seraphic catalyst.

Where fates transpire
And predetermined events manifest.

Mark the calendar
Jot the dates.

To swim with
The lunar current.

Do your lunar magic!

Your lunar magic sparkles
With magical air.

Where wishes are heard
And dreams come true.

15. The Lovers Card Reversed

In tarot and in life,
Your lovers!
Did they ever think about you?
Ask you what you wanted?

Did they ever pay attention to your needs?
Or was it all about them?
Did they consider you before making decisions?
Or ask your thoughts on what the future would look
like?

Did they feel what you felt?
The pain of being left behind?
Being away but still waiting?
Did love not carry you through trials and quests?
Then it's not love!

The Lovers card reversed!
Tension and turmoil.

Disagreements in the slightest.
Butting heads at every corner.
Disharmony everywhere.

Yet you think love will carry you through.
But love can't make another heart sing for you.
If it's not meant to be, it's not meant to be.
Individuality cannot be sacrificed at anyone's expense.

But if it's meant to be, then love will find a way.
For there's a union of hearts and ties of souls.
The stars will make a way
So that destinies can align and souls can unite.

16. Rose Gardens

Take me to rose gardens,
Where there's beauty and love,
And perfumes of spring blooms.
Roses far and wide,
And scenic charm all around.

I place a rose behind my ear,
Rosé in my hand,
Walking down memory lane.
Thinking about
The sweetest memories with you.

Feeling the highs
From a newfound love,
And euphoric from
Every dialogue we shared,
While strolling through rose gardens.

Lingering shivers that keep me
Coming for more.

Sleepless nights,
And misplaced appetite.
Like a sugar rush,
Or a cocaine high.

Dreaming of the very first time
We met in a rose garden,
In your city;
Where your brown eyes
Met mine for the first time.

The instant fondness of hearts,
And the undeniable pull of heartstrings
From the very first moment
That led to quick exchanges
And long conversations.

I have the most beautiful reflections
Reminiscing about nostalgic glimpses
In a rose garden
With you by my side.

17. Mercury

Ruled by the planet Mercury
His wit and comic sense of humor
Was the finest I've ever seen.
His gregarious and animated character
Lights up the room.

His lively laughs
And overly friendly conversations
Makes everyone bewitched
And fascinated.

He takes you on a trip to Wonderland
Where things are young
And fun again.

That youthful blood
Kicks in again.
Merriment and frolly
All around anew.

Like you're seven all over again.
Head spinning with mirth and glee.
Head in the stars and feet off the ground.

His tales - gripping and heart-stopping
That allows you to picture every scene
He recounts, scene by scene.

Pin it on Mercury for making its signs
Witty and fun-loving;
Versatile and eccentric.

Like Hermes,
The God of planet Mercury;
The God of communication.

Known for his exquisite
Communication skills;
Blessed its signs
With quick wit and astute.

18. Genie In The Lamp

Genie in the lamp,
Make my wishes come true.
In life as in dreams,
May I find my one true love
To sing away into forever.

Genie in the lamp,
Please answer my prayers.
I wish for a lover
To spend my days and nights
With love and happiness and laughter.

Genie in the lamp,
I make another wish.
Take me to the Blue Lagoon,
Where there's crystal blue waters underneath
And the ocean breeze around me.

Genie in the lamp,
This is my last wish

That you live in love and laughter
And freedom forever and ever
Into eternity.

No longer a genie in the lamp,
I set you free
To roam the world
From one farthest end to the other.
No longer in bondage.
No longer am I your Master.

I break the curse
Once and for all.
And set you loose
To do as you please
And enjoy all the years you've missed,
Bound as a genie in the lamp.

19. Dear Italy

Dear Italy,
Your vibes, your laughter,
And your love echoes
Forever in my mind.

The way you live your life
So unapologetic and loud.
And how you make me
Feel right at home.

Your sunny days
And chilly nights;
Your stunning islands
And the Mediterranean Sea,
All make me so nostalgic.

Dear Italy,
Your food, your local produce,
Cannot get fresher than this.
Love echoes through every dish.

Your friendly people
And warm hugs,
Makes my day
Into one of sunshine and clear skies.

20. Notebook

Dear notebook,
You've been my spine
On days I lacked some,
And my therapist
On rainy days.

You've been my cheerer
On days I needed it the most.
My scheduler,
Organising my days
When I couldn't keep track of my time.

Dear notebook,
On some days,
You've been my tissue
Where I've shed tears
In wretchedness.

You've been a carrier
Of all my poems

Written always with good faith
And gospel truth.

You've been a bearer
Of good news and fortune
On days when I struck gold;
The good days
When heaven struck me.

You've been my best friend
Yesterday, today,
And will be, tomorrow
And into eternity
Till my soul parts away.

21. Cherry On Top

Mom,
You're the cherry on top
Of my icing of a life.

You've made my days better,
And my nights sublime.
You've been my rock-solid, do-or-die

Through thick and through thin,
Through frolic and through sorrow,
You've always stood by me..

You showed me by example
What love is,
And what patience is.

You're my cherry on top,
Making everything better
Just by existing.

By being an example,
You led me
In work and in life.

Your unconditional love for me
Is what's moulded me
Into the person I am.

Your willingness to live life
Fearlessly and all-in
Taught me how to play
This game of life.

By acts of kindness
And deeds of probity
You showed me the path -
The good life.

You're my cherry on top,
Giving my life meaning
And love.